D1097635

# IMPRESSIONISM

◆

# POST-IMPRESSIONISM

*Masterpieces from the* MUSÉE D'ORSAY

Musée
d'Orsay

SAN FRANCISCO

de Young

Fine Arts
Museums of
San Francisco

Pomegranate Communications, Inc.
Box 808022, Petaluma CA 94975
800 227 1428; www.pomegranate.com

Pomegranate Europe Ltd.
Unit 1, Heathcote Business Centre, Hurlbutt Road
Warwick, Warwickshire CV34 6TD, UK
[+44] 0 1926 430111; sales@pomeurope.co.uk

ISBN 978-0-7649-5497-9
Pomegranate Catalog No. AA644

Pomegranate publishes books of postcards on a wide range of subjects.
Please contact the publisher for more information.

Cover designed by Patrice Morris
Printed in Korea
19 18 17 16 15 14 13 12 11 10     10 9 8 7 6 5 4 3 2 1

To facilitate detachment of the postcards from this book, fold each card along its perforation line before tearing.

B eginning in the early 1860s, a group of French realist painters rejected the standards and traditions of the Académie des Beaux-Arts and struck out on their own, developing a new style that favored plein air renditions of landscapes and scenes from everyday life. The Impressionists, as these artists and their followers came to be called, used their new approach in painting to capture the fleeting effects of weather and light, achieving vivid, realistic effects through luminous color and animated brushwork.

Coined in the early 1900s, the term *Post-Impressionism* refers to an artistic movement that pushed the daring departures of Impressionism even further. Inspired by the likes of Monet and Pissarro, Post-Impressionist painters relied on visible brushstrokes and thickly applied paint, but they rejected the naturalistic heritage of Impressionism in favor of greater expressiveness—a freer use of color and a step or two further from photographic realism. Although they often exhibited together, the Post-Impressionists never mustered a collective creed and were happy to set off along divergent stylistic paths. Their experimentation led the way toward Cubism and Fauvism—two major artistic movements of the early twentieth century.

The Musée d'Orsay, a train station created for the Paris International Exposition of 1900 and transformed into a museum by renowned architect Gae Aulenti, opened to the public on December 9, 1986, with its goal to highlight the art of the Western world from the period 1848 through 1914. Its collection comprises paintings, sculpture, drawings, decorative arts, furniture, photography, and architectural work from this period. The Musée d'Orsay's collection of Impressionist and Post-Impressionist paintings represents the finest survey of its kind in the world.

The thirty paintings reproduced in this book of postcards represent highlights of the Impressionist and Post-Impressionist movements. All are from the unparalleled collection of the Musée d'Orsay. ✦

# Impressionism · Post-Impressionism

Pierre-Auguste Renoir (1841–1919)
*The Swing,* 1876
Oil on canvas, 92 x 73 cm (36¼ x 28¾ in.)
Musée d'Orsay, RF 2738
Photograph © RMN (Musée d'Orsay) / Hervé Lewandowski

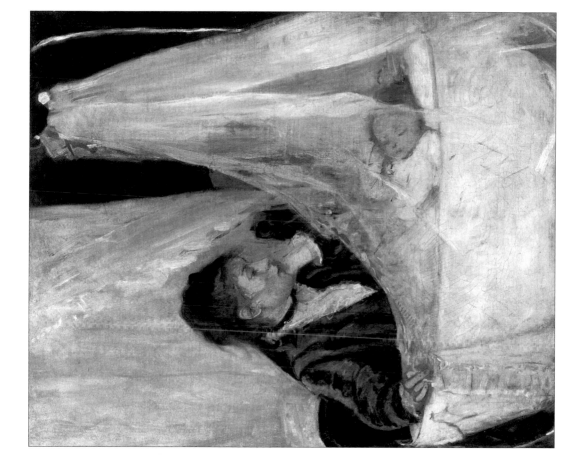

# Impressionism · Post-Impressionism

Berthe Morisot (1841–1895)

*The Cradle,* 1872
Oil on canvas, 56 x 46 cm (22 x 18⅛ in.)
Musée d'Orsay, RF 2849
Photograph © RMN (Musée d'Orsay) / Hervé Lewandowski

# IMPRESSIONISM · POST-IMPRESSIONISM

Georges Lemmen (1865–1916)

*Beach at Heist,* 1891
Oil on canvas, 37.5 x 46 cm (14¾ x 18⅛ in.)
Musée d'Orsay, RF 1987 35
Photograph © RMN (Musée d'Orsay) / Gérard Blot

WWW.POMEGRANATE.COM

707 782 9000

Pomegranate

# Impressionism · Post-Impressionism

Vincent van Gogh (1853–1890)

*Starry Night over the Rhone,* 1888
Oil on canvas, 72.5 x 92 cm (28½ x 36¼ in.)
Musée d'Orsay, RF 1975 19
Photograph © RMN (Musée d'Orsay) / Hervé Lewandowski

707 782 9000  WWW.POMEGRANATE.COM

Pomegranate

# IMPRESSIONISM · POST-IMPRESSIONISM

Maurice Denis (1870–1943)
*Young Women at the Lamp,* 1891
Oil on canvas, 36 x 65 cm (14 x 25½ in.)
Musée d'Orsay, RF 2001 10
Photograph © RMN (Musée d'Orsay) / Hervé Lewandowski
© Artists Rights Society (ARS), New York / ADAGP, Paris

# Impressionism · Post-Impressionism

Frédéric Bazille (1841–1870)

*Family Reunion,* 1867
Oil on canvas, 152 x 230 cm (59⅞ x 90½ in.)
Musée d'Orsay, RF 2749
Photograph © RMN (Musée d'Orsay) / Hervé Lewandowski

707 782 9000   WWW.POMEGRANATE.COM

Pomegranate

# Impressionism · Post-Impressionism

Vincent van Gogh (1853–1890)
*Van Gogh's Bedroom at Arles,* 1889
Oil on canvas, 57.5 x 74 cm (22⅝ x 29⅛ in.)
Musée d'Orsay, RF 1959 2
Photograph © RMN (Musée d'Orsay) / Hervé Lewandowski

707 782 9000   WWW.POMEGRANATE.COM

# Impressionism · Post-Impressionism

Paul Cézanne (1839–1906)

*Still Life with Soup Tureen,* ca. 1877
Oil on canvas, 65 x 83 cm (25¼ x 32⅛ in.)
Musée d'Orsay, RF 2818
Photograph © RMN (Musée d'Orsay) / Hervé Lewandowski

707 782 9000   WWW.POMEGRANATE.COM

Pomegranate

# Impressionism · Post-Impressionism

Paul Gauguin (1848–1903)

*Breton Peasants,* 1894
Oil on canvas, 66 x 92.5 cm (26 x 36⅜ in.)
Musée d'Orsay, RF 1973 17
Photograph © RMN (Musée d'Orsay) / Hervé Lewandowski

WWW.POMEGRANATE.COM

707 782 9000

Pomegranate

# Impressionism · Post-Impressionism

Félix Vallotton (1865–1925)
*The Ball,* or *Corner of the Park with Child Playing with a Ball,* 1899
Oil on card, laid on wood panel, 48 x 61 cm (18⅞ x 24 in.)
Musée d'Orsay, RF 1977 353
Photograph © RMN (Musée d'Orsay) / Hervé Lewandowski

707 782 9000   WWW.POMEGRANATE.COM

Pomegranate

# Impressionism · Post-Impressionism

Edouard Manet (1832–1883)

*The Fifer,* 1866
Oil on canvas, 161 x 97 cm (63⅜ x 38¼ in.)
Musée d'Orsay, RF 1992
Photograph © RMN (Musée d'Orsay) / Hervé Lewandowski

707 782 9000   WWW.POMEGRANATE.COM

Pomegranate

# Impressionism · Post-Impressionism

James Abbott McNeill Whistler (1834–1903)
*Arrangement in Gray and Black No. 1* [also known as *Portrait of the Artist's Mother*], 1871
Oil on canvas, 144.3 x 162.5 cm (56¾ x 64 in.)
Musée d'Orsay, RF 699
Photograph © RMN (Musée d'Orsay) / Jean-Gilles Berizzi

# Impressionism · Post-Impressionism

Alfred Sisley (1839–1899)

*The Moret Bridge,* 1893
Oil on canvas, 73.5 x 92.5 cm (29 x 36¾ in.)
Musée d'Orsay, RF 1972 35
Photograph © RMN (Musée d'Orsay) / Hervé Lewandowski

707 782 9000   WWW.POMEGRANATE.COM

Pomegranate

# Impressionism · Post-Impressionism

Henri Rousseau (1844–1910)
*The Snake Charmer,* 1907
Oil on canvas, 169 x 189.5 cm (66½ x 74⅝ in.)
Musée d'Orsay, RF 1937 7
Photograph © RMN (Musée d'Orsay) / Hervé Lewandowski

707 782 9000   WWW.POMEGRANATE.COM

Pomegranate

# Impressionism · Post-Impressionism

Camille Pissarro (1830–1903)
*Young Peasant Girl Starting a Fire: Hoarfrost,* 1888
Oil on canvas, 92.8 x 92.5 cm (36⅝ x 36½ in.)
Musée d'Orsay, RF 2000 83
Photograph © RMN (Musée d'Orsay) / Hervé Lewandowski

# Impressionism · Post-Impressionism

Claude Monet (1840–1926)

*The Magpie,* 1868
Oil on canvas, 89 x 130 cm (35 x 51⅛ in.)
Musée d'Orsay, RF 1984 164
Photograph © RMN (Musée d'Orsay) / Hervé Lewandowski

707 782 9000  WWW.POMEGRANATE.COM

Pomegranate

# Impressionism · Post-Impressionism

Gustave Caillebotte (1848–1894)

*The Floor Scrapers,* 1875
Oil on canvas, 102 x 146.5 cm (40⅛ x 57⅝ in.)
Musée d'Orsay, RF 2718
Photograph © RMN (Musée d'Orsay) / Hervé Lewandowski

707 782 9000   WWW.POMEGRANATE.COM

Pomegranate

# Impressionism · Post-Impressionism

Paul Cézanne (1839–1906)
*The Gulf of Marseille Seen from L'Estaque,* ca. 1878–1879
Oil on canvas, 58 x 72 cm (22½ x 28¼ in.)
Musée d'Orsay, RF 2761
Photograph © RMN (Musée d'Orsay) / Thierry le Mage

707 782 9000    WWW.POMEGRANATE.COM

Pomegranate

# Impressionism · Post-Impressionism

Edgar Degas (1834–1917)
*Race Horses before the Stands,* ca. 1866–1868
Oil on cardboard on canvas, 46 x 61 cm (18⅛ x 24 in.)
Musée d'Orsay, RF 1981
Photograph © RMN (Musée d'Orsay) / Hervé Lewandowski

WWW.POMEGRANATE.COM   707 782 9000

Pomegranate

# IMPRESSIONISM · POST-IMPRESSIONISM

Claude Monet (1840–1926)
*Rue Montorgueil, Paris, Festival of June 30, 1878,* 1878
Oil on canvas, 81 x 50.5 cm (31⅞ x 19⅞ in.)
Musée d'Orsay, RF 1982 71
Photograph © RMN (Musée d'Orsay) / Hervé Lewandowski

707 782 9000   WWW.POMEGRANATE.COM

Pomegranate

# IMPRESSIONISM · POST-IMPRESSIONISM

Alfred Stevens (1823–1906)

*The Bath,* ca. 1897
Oil on canvas, 76 x 93 cm (30 x 37 in.)
Musée d'Orsay, 1926 (INV 20846)
Photograph © RMN (Musée d'Orsay) / Hervé Lewandowski

707 782 9000   WWW.POMEGRANATE.COM

Pomegranate

# Impressionism · Post-Impressionism

Odilon Redon (1840–1916)

*The Sleep of Caliban,* 1895–1900
Oil on wood, 48.3 x 38.5 cm (19 x 15¼ in.)
Musée d'Orsay, RF 1984 48
Photograph © RMN (Musée d'Orsay) / Hervé Lewandowski

WWW.POMEGRANATE.COM

707 782 9000

Pomegranate

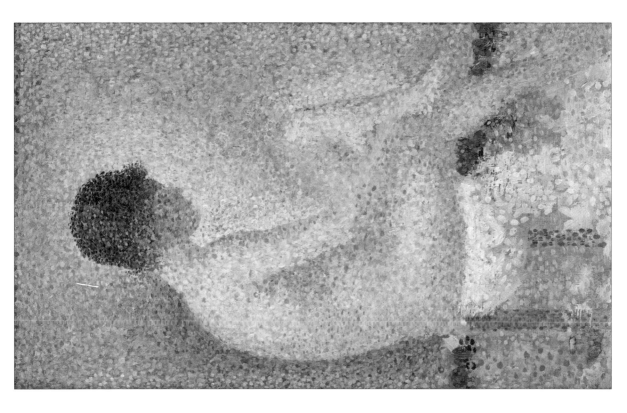

# IMPRESSIONISM · POST-IMPRESSIONISM

Georges Seurat (1859–1891)

*Model, Profile View,* 1887
Oil on wood, 25 x 16 cm (9⅞ x 6¼ in.)
Musée d'Orsay, RF 1947 14
Photograph © RMN (Musée d'Orsay) / René-Gabriel Ojéda

# Impressionism · Post-Impressionism

Thèo van Rysselberghe (1862–1926)
*Man at the Helm,* 1892
Oil on canvas, 60.2 x 80.3 cm (23¾ x 31⅝ in.)
Musée d'Orsay, RF 1976 79
Photograph © RMN (Musée d'Orsay) / Hervé Lewandowski

WWW.POMEGRANATE.COM

707 782 9000

Pomegranate

# Impressionism · Post-Impressionism

Paul Sérusier (1864–1927)
*The Flowery Barrier,* 1889
Oil on canvas, 73 x 60 cm (28¾ x 23⅝ in.)
Musée d'Orsay, RF 1980 52
Photograph © RMN (Musée d'Orsay) / Hervé Lewandowski

707 782 9000   WWW.POMEGRANATE.COM

Pomegranate

# Impressionism · Post-Impressionism

Claude Monet (1840–1926)
*The Turkeys: Château of Rottembourg at Montgeron,* 1877
Oil on canvas, 174.5 x 172.5 cm (68¾ x 67⅞ in.)
Musée d'Orsay, RF 1944 18
Photograph © RMN (Musée d'Orsay) / Hervé Lewandowski

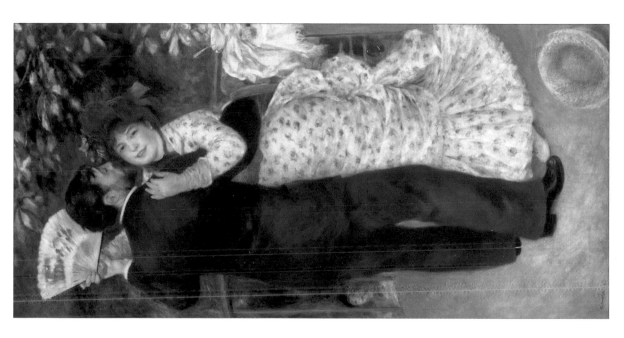

# Impressionism · Post-Impressionism

Pierre-Auguste Renoir (1841–1919)

*A Dance in the Country,* 1883
Oil on canvas, 180 x 90 cm (70⅞ x 35½ in.)
Musée d'Orsay, RF 1979 64
Photograph © RMN (Musée d'Orsay) / Hervé Lewandowski

707 782 9000   WWW.POMEGRANATE.COM

Pomegranate

# Impressionism · Post-Impressionism

Georges Seurat (1859–1891)
Study for *A Bathing Place at Asnières,* 1883
Oil on wood, 15.5 x 25 cm (6⅛ x 9⅞ in.)
Musée d'Orsay, RF 1965 13
Photograph © RMN (Musée d'Orsay) / Hervé Lewandowski

WWW.POMEGRANATE.COM

707 782 9000

*Pomegranate*

# Impressionism · Post-Impressionism

Paul Signac (1863–1935)
*Entry to the Port of Marseille,* 1918–1920
Oil on canvas, 116.5 x 162.5 cm (45¾ x 64 in.)
Musée d'Orsay, RF 1977 324
Photograph © RMN (Musée d'Orsay)

707 782 9000   WWW.POMEGRANATE.COM

Pomegranate

# Impressionism · Post-Impressionism

William-Adolphe Bouguereau (1825–1905)

*Birth of Venus,* 1879
Oil on canvas, 300 x 215 cm (118⅛ x 84⅝ in.)
Musée d'Orsay, RF 253
Photograph © RMN (Musée d'Orsay) / Hervé Lewandowski

707 782 9000   WWW.POMEGRANATE.COM

Pomegranate